DRAGONFLY

Garden Minibeasts UP CLOSE

John Woodward

CHELSEA CLUBHOUSE
An Imprint of Chelsea House Publishers

Dragonfly

Chelsea Clubhouse
An imprint of Chelsea House
132 West 31st Street
New York, NY 10001

Library of Congress Cataloging-in-Publication Data
Woodward, John.
Dragonfly / John Woodward.
p. cm. -- (Garden minibeasts up close)
Includes index.
ISBN 978-1-60413-898-6
1. Dragonflies--Juvenile literature. I. Title. II. Series: Woodward, John, 1954- Garden minibeasts up close.
QL520.W66 2010
595.7'33--dc22
2009052774

Chelsea Clubhouse books are available at special discounts when purchased in bulk quantities for businesses, associations, institutions, or sales promotions. Please call our Special Sales Department in New York at (212) 967-8800 or (800) 322-8755.

You can find Chelsea Clubhouse on the World Wide Web at http://www.chelseahouse.com

Produced for Chelsea House by Discovery Books
Managing Editor: Laura Durman
Project Editor: Clare Collinson
Designer: Blink Media
Illustrator: Stuart Lafford

Photo acknowledgments: Corbis: pp 7 (Layne Kennedy), 18 (Naturfoto Honal); FLPA: pp 13, 14, and 17 (Michael Durham/ Minden Pictures), 19 and 20 (ImageBroker/Imagebroker), 24 (Rene Krekels/FN/Minden); iStockphoto.com: pp 4 (Megan Stevens), 9 (John Anderson), 10 (Vladimir Eskin), 15 (ruchos), 16 (sebastien barrau), 23 (Michel de Nijs), 28 (Patricia Casanave), 29 (Kim Murrell); Photoshot: p 25 (NHPA); Shutterstock Images: title page (Vlad Turchenko), pp 5 (John A. Anderson), 8 (orionmystery@flickr), 11 (jpatava), 12 (Akvile Rakstyte), 21 (Doug Lemke), 22 (William Attard McCarthy), 26 top and bottom (vblinov), 27 top and bottom (vblinov).

Cover printed by Bang Printing, Brainerd, MN
Book printed and bound by Bang Printing, Brainerd, MN
Date printed April 2010
Printed in the United States of America

10 9 8 7 6 5 4 3 2 1

This book is printed on acid-free paper.

Contents

Finding dragonflies

Have you ever seen a fast-flying insect darting this way and that over water? It was probably a dragonfly. Dragonflies usually live near **freshwater**, where they lay their eggs. You can find them by rivers, streams, lakes, and ponds.

A flame skimmer perches by a pond, looking for insects to eat.

This amberwing dragonfly is resting on a flower in someone's backyard.

Did You Know?

Some dragonflies prefer to live near ponds with hardly any plants in them. They are often the first animals that turn up to investigate newly dug backyard ponds.

Adult dragonflies are strong fliers. They can often be found a long way from water, and they regularly visit backyards. You may see one zooming around in search of insects to eat, or perching on a plant or fence.

The best time to see dragonflies is in the summer. Adult dragonflies cannot survive cold weather.

A dragonfly's body

One of the first things you notice about a dragonfly is its long, slender body.

A dragonfly has two large eyes that almost cover its head, a bit like a motorcycle helmet! It has two pairs of long, thin wings.

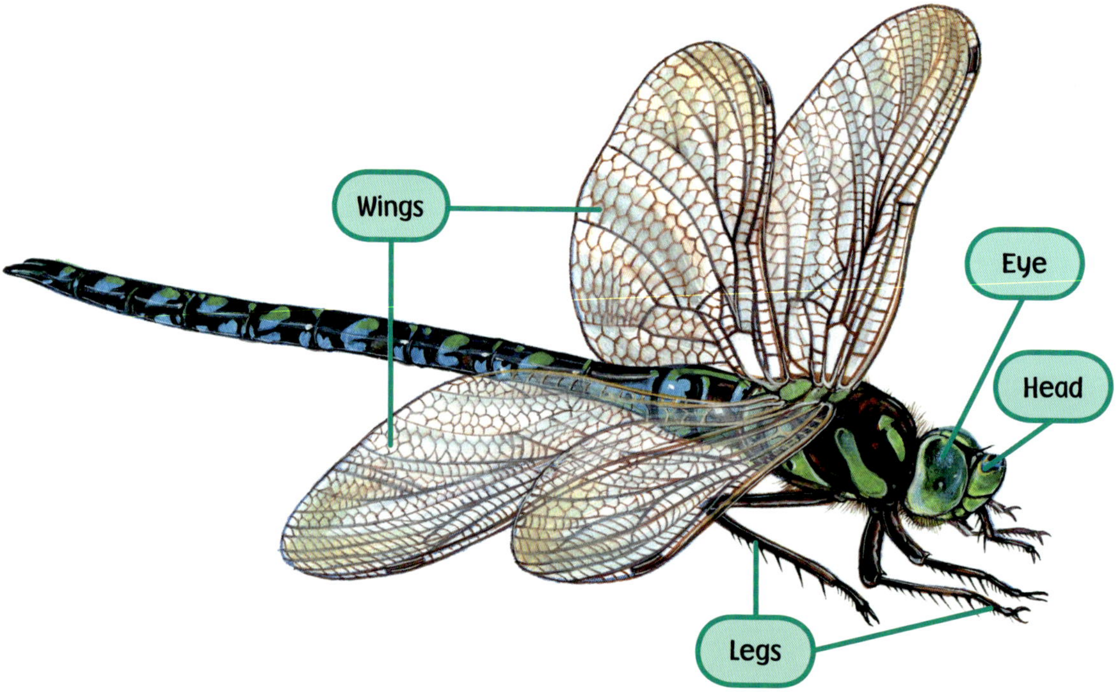

Like other insects, a dragonfly has six legs. Its legs are specially shaped to help it catch insects while it is flying. Dragonflies also use their legs to perch on plants and stones, but they cannot walk.

Did You Know?

Dragonflies have lived on Earth for at least 300 million years—that's 70 million years before the first dinosaurs! Some early dragonflies had a **wingspan** of 30 inches. Today most dragonflies have a wingspan that is between 1 and 4 inches.

This **fossil** shows the remains of a dragonfly that lived millions of years ago.

Amazing eyes

It's hard to sneak up on a dragonfly without being noticed! All dragonflies have fantastic vision. They have huge **compound eyes** made up of thousands of tiny **lenses**. Each lens helps the dragonfly to form a detailed picture of what is nearby.

Dragonflies have the biggest eyes in the insect world. Their eyes often meet at the top of their heads.

The lenses in a dragonfly's eyes face in all directions. This gives it an all-around view of its surroundings. A dragonfly's eyes are particularly good at sensing movement. This helps the dragonfly spot small insects when it is hunting.

Did You Know?

Dragonflies have up to 30,000 tiny lenses in each eye! Humans have only one lens in each eye.

Like all dragonflies, this green darner depends on its eyes for hunting. Dragonflies can sense the movements of insects up to 40 feet away!

Damselflies

If you visit a pond or river in summer, look out for a delicate, fluttery insect, with colors that glow like neon lights. You may think it is a small dragonfly, but in fact it is a damselfly. Damselfies are closely related to dragonflies and they look very similar. How can you tell them apart?

A brightly colored, dainty damselfly perches with its wings closed over the top of its body.

A damselfly has smaller eyes than a dragonfly. Its eyes are wide apart, on either side of its head.

When dragonflies rest on a perch, they keep their wings stretched out. Damselflies perch with their wings folded back over their bodies.

Damselflies are weaker flyers than dragonflies and they have thinner bodies. A dragonfly's big eyes often touch at the top of its head. A damselfly has eyes that are widely separated.

Did You Know?

Most damselflies are smaller than dragonflies. But helicopter damselflies of South and Central America are bigger than any dragonfly. They have a wingspan of over seven inches!

Wings and flying

If you watch a dragonfly hunting insects, you will be amazed by its flying skills. Dragonflies can fly very fast and turn almost instantly. They can dart straight up and down, hover, and even fly backward.

A dragonfly's delicate wings are very strong. They have a network of veins running through them. This makes the wings stiff and tough.

Why are dragonflies such skilful flyers? Unlike most other insects, they can flap their front and back wings separately from each other. This gives them better control when they are flying.

Did You Know?

The official speed record for a dragonfly is 36 miles per hour (mph). That may not sound like much, but considering its size, it is like a pigeon flying at 160 mph!

Dragonflies have powerful muscles to help them control each wing separately.

Airborne hunters

A whitetail dragonfly flies through the air, ready to capture insects with its legs.

Dragonflies are fierce hunters. They eat all sorts of small flying insects, such as flies, bees, and butterflies. They especially like to eat mosquitoes.

A dragonfly uses its big eyes to target its **prey**. Then it chases after it at high speed.

Did You Know?

Some large dragonflies are powerful enough to catch and eat small frogs. They zoom down low and pluck them from the ground.

This clubtail dragonfly has caught a bee. It has settled on a plant to eat its prey.

When a dragonfly gets close to its victim, it pushes its legs forward to make a "basket." Then it scoops up the insect in mid-air.

Large dragonflies may eat their prey in flight. Others land on a perch to eat their meal.

Ambush and patrol

Different types of dragonfly have different ways of hunting. Some rest on a perch and watch for flying insects to come their way. When they spot their prey, they dart up and **ambush** it in the air.

A hungry Halloween pennant gets ready to launch itself into the air to chase a passing fly.

Did You Know?

Large dragonflies sometimes attack smaller dragonflies and damselflies that stray into their path while on patrol.

Darner dragonflies spend most of the day flying about hunting insects.

Some large dragonflies prefer to **patrol** an area in flight. They fly up and down, twisting in the air to snatch any insects that come near. But even these more active hunters sometimes stop on a perch to rest.

Males and females

A male damselfly has attracted a female to its territory. Male damselflies often have darker wings than females.

Male dragonflies are usually more brightly colored than females. They often appear more active, too. Their job is to find a good place to **breed** and attract a female to their **territory**. They must also defend their territory from other males.

These three rival males are competing for a good breeding site.

Sometimes many males fight to gain control of a good breeding site. These combats can get serious. The **rivals** dart and dive at each other. They may even clash in midair.

Did You Know?

Sometimes fights between male dragonflies result in one rival being knocked into the water, where it is likely to be eaten by a fish.

Mating pairs

If you see two dragonflies clinging together in mid-air, they are probably a **mating** pair. When a male attracts a female to his territory, he seizes her with his legs. Then he clings to the back of her head with special claws on the tip of his body.

A male dragonfly has attached himself to a female before they mate. They are flying together in **tandem**.

Did You Know?

When they mate, male dragonflies often cling to a female's neck for an hour or more. Some dragonflies mate as they fly. Others settle on waterside plants to mate.

The female curls her body under the male's, forming a "wheel" position. This allows the pair to mate and the male **fertilizes** the female's eggs.

Two ebony jewelwing damselflies mate in the wheel position. The male is on the left and the female on the right.

Laying eggs

When you see a dragonfly flying low over water, watch carefully. You may see it laying its eggs.

Some female dragonflies simply drop their eggs into water as they hover close to the surface. Others carefully inject their eggs into floating plants, or soft mud near the water.

A green darner is injecting its eggs into the stem of a water plant.

A male damselfly clings to a female as she lays her eggs. This gives her extra wing power if she needs to escape from enemies such as frogs.

As the female lays her eggs, the male guards her from other males. He may even cling to the back of the female's head.

Did You Know?

Some female damselflies dive underwater to lay their eggs. They breathe air that they have trapped between their wings. They may stay underwater for more than an hour as they lay their eggs!

Hungry young

A few weeks or months after they have been laid, dragonfly eggs hatch out into **larvae**. A dragonfly larva does not look much like its beautiful parents! It has no wings and is often colored to blend in with its surroundings.

Dragonfly larvae live underwater until they are fully grown. As they grow, they shed their tough skin every time it gets too tight.

This young dragonfly larva is living among the plants in a pond. It can be up to four years before a larva is fully grown.

Like its parents, a dragonfly larva is a fierce hunter. It preys on **tadpoles**, small fish, and insects that live underwater. Dragonfly larvae have powerful jaws and sharp teeth.

Did You Know?

Many dragonfly larvae squirt water out of their back ends to help them move quickly through the water. They do this to escape from enemies and to catch their prey!

Some large dragonfly larvae, such as this darner, are strong enough to catch fish.

Airborne!

Have you ever found an empty insect skin near a pond or lake? It was probably left there by a dragonfly larva.

When a larva is fully grown, it climbs up a water plant and clings on while it dries out. Then it splits open at the back and gradually an adult dragonfly comes out. This process is called **metamorphosis**.

At first the dragonfly's body is short and its wings are crumpled. Slowly it pumps itself up and finally spreads its wings. Then suddenly it takes off and flies away.

An adult dragonfly gradually emerges, leaving the larva's skin behind.

Did You Know?

When it emerges, an adult dragonfly has very little color. This acts as **camouflage**. The dragonfly is hidden from enemies at a time when it cannot escape. Its color develops slowly over the next few days.

Dragonflies and people

Dragonflies are fierce hunters and you may think they look a bit scary. However, they are completely harmless to humans. They do not bite or sting us. They are also useful because they eat insects that are harmful to humans, such as mosquitoes.

If a dragonfly lands on your hand, look closely at it. It will not hurt you.

Green darners are among the largest and fastest flying dragonflies in North America.

Did You Know?

In the southern United States the green darner dragonfly is sometimes called the "snake doctor." People once believed that it followed snakes around and stitched them back together if they were injured!

In some countries, dragonflies once had a bad **reputation**. A traditional English name for dragonflies was "devil's **darning** needles." In some parts of South America they were called "horse killers."

However, in Japan dragonflies are **symbols** of courage, strength, and happiness. To some Native Americans they represent swiftness and activity.

Glossary

ambush: Make a surprise attack on something.

breed: Multiply by producing young.

camouflage: Type of coloring or shape that makes something hard to see against its background.

compound eye: A bundle of many very simple eyes that act together to form a picture. All adult insects have this type of eye.

darning: A type of sewing, used to mend holes in knitted clothes such as socks.

fertilize: In animals, to add the material that makes an egg develop into a baby.

fossil: The remains of an ancient creature preserved in rock.

freshwater: Water that is not obviously salty, as in ponds, rivers, and most lakes.

larva: The young life stage of an insect, when it does most of its feeding. Plural is larvae.

lens: See-through structure in the eye that focuses light to form a picture in the brain.

mating: When males and females come together to produce young.

metamorphosis: Turning into another form, as when a caterpillar turns into a butterfly.

patrol: Regularly move around an area to keep watch for something.

prey: An animal that is attacked and eaten by another animal.

reputation: What people think about something or someone, whether it is true or not.

rival: Another animal (or person) who wants the same thing, and is prepared to fight for it in some way.

symbol: A thing that stands for something else.

tadpole: The young form of a frog or toad, which lives underwater.

tandem: Arranged one behind the other.

territory: In animals, an area that is claimed as a feeding or breeding site. It is usually claimed by the male but not always.

wingspan: The width across an animal's wings measured from tip to tip.

Further resources

Books

Nikula, Blair, Jackie Sones, Donald Stokes, and Lillian Stokes. *Stokes Beginner's Guide to Dragonflies.* New York: Little, Brown and Company, 2002.
A colorful, simple-to-use guide to dragonflies, containing photographs of the most common species.

Prischmann, Deirdre A. *Dragonflies.* Bloomington: Capstone Press, 2006.
An introduction to the nature, habitats, life cycles, and enemies of dragonflies.

Slade, Suzanne. *Dragonflies.* New York: Rosen Publishing, 2008.
An interesting guide to dragonflies containing photographs taken using a microscope.

St Pierre, Stephanie. *Dragonfly.* Chicago: Heinemann Library, 2008.
A close look at what makes dragonflies special, including how they grow, feed, move, and breed.

Web sites

A beginner's guide to dragonflies, ***http://www.kaweahoaks.com/html/dragonflies.htm***
This Web site contains lots of information for readers who want to know more.

Biokids, "Dragonflies," ***http://www.biokids.umich.edu/critters/Anisoptera***
Aimed at young people, this introduction to dragonflies has plenty of information for the reader who has a few unanswered questions.

Digital dragonflies, ***http://www.dragonflies.org***
This Web site contains a collection of detailed pictures of American dragonflies and a lot of useful information.

Dragonfly site, ***http://www.dragonfly-site.com***
This useful Web site is full of information about dragonflies and includes a picture gallery of American dragonflies.

Index